Narcissa Whitman

BRAVE PIONEER

Library of Congress Cataloging in Publication Data

Sabin, Louis.
  Narcissa Whitman, brave pioneer.

    Summary: Focuses on events from youth of a missionary
who was the first white woman to cross the Rocky
Mountains.
    1. Whitman, Narcissa Prentiss, 1808-1847—Juvenile
literature. 2. Nez Perce Indians—Missions—Juvenile
literature. 3. Missionaries—Northwest, Pacific—Biography—Juvenile literature. 4. Indians of North America
—Northwest, Pacific—Missions—Juvenile literature.
5. Pioneers—Northwest, Pacific—Biography—Juvenile
literature. 6. Northwest, Pacific—Biography—Juvenile
literature. [1. Whitman, Narcissa Prentiss, 1808-1847.
2. Missionaries] I. Eitzen, Allan, ill. II. Title.
E99.N5W447   979.5 '03 '0924 [B] [92]   81-23066
ISBN 0-89375-762-4   AACR2
ISBN 0-89375-763-2 (pbk.)

Narcissa Whitman

BRAVE PIONEER

Caroline and Charles Ingalls were Laura's parents.

Laura and her family moved many times. Pa always wanted to move out west and **settle** new land. When Laura was two, they moved west to the flat prairie of Kansas.

The Ingalls family traveled in a covered wagon pulled by horses. At night, they camped by the wagon. They made a fire to keep warm and to use for cooking. They slept under the stars. When it rained, the family huddled in the wagon. It was hard to move the whole family in a covered wagon.

Many people moved west in covered wagons.

7

The Kansas prairie land was very different from Wisconsin. It was flat and dry. Tall grasses blew back and forth in the winds. There were no hills and very few trees. The winters were long, and there were many storms. It was harder to farm on the prairie than in Wisconsin.

The Ingalls family lived in a log house that Pa had built. At night Pa played the **fiddle** to make everyone laugh and sing. In time, they began to get used to living in Kansas. Then Laura's father learned that they could have their Wisconsin land back. So the family moved back to the big woods.

Charles Ingalls built a log house much like this one.

They only stayed one year in Wisconsin. When Laura was seven, Pa moved the family to Minnesota and started a farm. There they lived in a little **dugout** house. It was built into the side of a hill by a creek. It had one door and one window. The roof was made of **sod**. Once, a cow stepped through the roof of their little home!

Laura and her sisters went to a one-room school in town. Pa grew tall fields of wheat. One day, many thousands of grasshoppers came through and ate all their **crops**. They could not save the farm. So the family had to move again. This time, they moved to nearby Iowa.

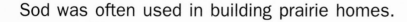
Sod was often used in building prairie homes.

Laura was happy in Iowa. Pa worked at a hotel in town. But he missed the wide open spaces of the country. Soon the Ingalls family moved back to Minnesota again.

There Laura's sister Mary got very sick. Mary had a high fever and almost died. She became blind. Pa asked Laura to promise to be Mary's eyes for her. After that, Laura always told Mary everything she saw.

Then Pa heard he could get a job working on the railroads. Soon the family moved again. This time, they traveled to South Dakota.

Carrie, Mary, and Laura Ingalls were very close.

Life in South Dakota was very hard. Summers were hot and the winters were freezing cold. One winter, a **blizzard** hit the town. Store owners had only kept a little food for sale in the stores. Soon that ran out. But the blizzard went on. Snow was so deep that people could not get out. No trains could get into town with food. People almost **starved** to death that long winter.

At last, a strong young man from Laura's town made it through the blizzard to another town. He brought back food for many people. His name was Almanzo Wilder. Laura liked this brave young man.

Laura Ingalls met Almanzo Wilder in South Dakota.

The little girl looked very serious as she worked. It was her job to sweep the front porch and steps every day. And she liked to do it well. She made sure every inch was as clean as a broom could make it. Not a bit of dirt was left when she was done.

Five-year-old Narcissa Prentiss liked to do grown-up jobs. She enjoyed helping her mother keep the house clean. It was a special treat to help her father at his sawmill, where he cut tree logs into boards. And she liked to go berry-picking with her brothers.

From the time Narcissa was born, on March 14, 1808, Mr. and Mrs. Prentiss knew she was special. A lovely, golden-haired child, she had a sweet temper and was a fast learner. When she was a baby, she was happy just to sit quietly and watch her mother cook, work at the spinning wheel, make candles, and bake bread. And as soon as she was old enough to walk, Narcissa began to do her share of the chores.

There were dozens of things to do every day in the Prentiss house. In those days, people living in villages like Prattsburg, New York, made almost everything they needed. There were no bakeries, food stores, or clothing stores. When people wanted bread, they had to grow the grain, grind it into flour, then bake it in their own oven. When they needed clothes, they made them. To do this, they grew flax in the field. Or they cut the wool from their sheep. Then they would spin their own linen or woolen thread, and weave it into cloth. Finally, the cloth was dyed, cut, and sewed into clothing.

Everyone in the family had to share in the work. Even a five-year-old, like Narcissa, had regular tasks. Just after sunrise every day, Mrs. Prentiss woke Narcissa, eight-year-old Stephen, and six-year-old Harvey. The children washed very quickly in their bedrooms and got dressed.

In those days, there were no indoor bathrooms. Instead, people pumped water from a well outside the house. They brought it into the house in buckets. Every evening, Stephen and Harvey brought in the water for the next day's washing. Then Narcissa helped the boys fill large pitchers to be put into each bedroom.

In the morning, Narcissa would pour some of the water from her pitcher into a large bowl. When the weather was warm, Narcissa was glad to use the cool, clear well water. But in the winter, washing was no fun at all. The water would freeze into a block of ice in the pitcher. Before she could wash, Narcissa had to chop up the ice and wait for it to melt.

After washing, the children scurried downstairs and out into the barnyard. Stephen helped Mr. Prentiss milk the cows. Narcissa and Harvey collected the eggs from the hens. Then they scattered seed over the ground for the chickens to eat. While the boys took care of the pigs and horses with Mr. Prentiss, Narcissa carried the eggs to her mother.

In the kitchen, a fire was blazing in the fireplace. Mrs. Prentiss was cutting bacon into strips. Narcissa's little brother Jonas was setting drinking mugs on the long wooden table.

Jonas hurried to finish setting the table. Then he went out to the shed behind the house. The maple syrup—from the sap of their own maple trees—was stored there, in a tall wooden tub. Near the bottom of the tub was a small wooden plug. Jonas pulled out the plug and held a bowl under the spout. Thick, golden syrup poured into the bowl. When it was full, Jonas plugged the hole. Then he carefully carried the syrup into the kitchen and put it on the table.

Narcissa set two pitchers on the table. They were brimming with fresh milk. A moment later, her mother asked her to mix the batter for the hot cakes. While Narcissa was busy with that, Mrs. Prentiss made porridge in a deep kettle, and fried bacon and sausages in an odd-looking frying pan called a "spider." The pan was black and stood on three long legs. These legs kept the bottom of the pan high above the fire. The pan looked like a long-legged spider, and that's just what people called it.

As soon as the sausages and bacon were cooked, Mrs. Prentiss told Narcissa to call everybody in for breakfast. "Hot cakes aren't much good if you don't eat them hot," Mrs. Prentiss said.

Narcissa dashed outside and met her father and brothers near the door. Mr. Prentiss and Stephen were carrying armloads of firewood. And little Harvey had a basket of twigs. These twigs would be used as kindling wood to start a fire.

The Prentiss family ate a huge breakfast every morning. They needed a hearty meal because they had already done a couple of hours of work before even sitting down at the table. And there were still plenty of chores to be done after breakfast, too.

The family wouldn't eat again until dinner, which usually was served in the afternoon. Then they would go back to work until supper.

18

Supper was a small meal, eaten at night. It might be cold corn cakes, porridge, or leftovers from dinner. Bedtime came early because everybody had to be up early the next morning to start the new day's chores.

The only day that was different was Sunday. After taking care of the animals, the men could look forward to a day of church-going and rest.

For the women, Sunday meant no weaving, spinning, churning butter, or grinding corn. But they were still expected to cook a good breakfast before church, and a fine dinner afterward.

This Sunday, Mrs. Prentiss and Narcissa wanted dinner to be extra fine. The Prentisses were to have very special guests that evening—

two men who had traveled west among the Indians.

Narcissa could barely contain her excitement as she helped her mother prepare the meal. "I want to hear every single one of their adventures. Do you think they'll tell us what it's like to be a pioneer?" she asked her mother.

"Yes, I do think so," said Mrs. Prentiss. "That is, if you give them half a chance to eat their dinners first!"

Narcissa was not disappointed that night. The two men were full of fascinating stories about the rugged trails leading west and about their work with the Indians. These men were missionaries. They hoped to help the Indians by teaching them to read and to farm, by sharing their faith with them, and by caring for the sick.

Every year, some teachers, doctors, and ministers traveled west. But it was a dangerous journey, and there were not many of these volunteers. Many who went did not return. Some died of illness. Some were killed by hostile Indians. Others lost their lives in floods and blizzards.

Narcissa listened carefully to the stories these men told. Dangerous though such work was, Narcissa told herself that one day she, too, would travel to this unknown territory to help others. What a great and worthy adventure it would be!

"When I'm grown up," she said to Stephen, "I shall be a pioneer and work among the Indians."

"What can *you* do?" he asked.

"I can be a teacher. I can run a school just like the one we go to," Narcissa said. "I'll have books for all the boys and girls. We'll have desks and slates to write on. We'll have quill pens and ink and writing paper. And I'll never take a birch rod to any of *my* pupils."

Narcissa liked learning. And she enjoyed school very much. The school she went to was a one-room cabin. All the pupils, who were between the ages of 5 and 12, sat in this room. The smallest ones sat up front, on long benches. They had no desks. The bigger children, sitting in rows behind them, shared rough wooden desks. The little boys and girls looked forward to being old enough to have a desk.

Their teacher was a strict young woman. Next to her desk stood a hollowed-out tree stump. In it, for all the class to see, were a dozen birch sticks. Any time a pupil misbehaved, the teacher called the child to the front of the room. Then, while everybody watched, the teacher hit the pupil's hand with two or three stinging swings of a birch stick.

In those days, it was common for teachers to keep order this way. To the children of that time, a good teacher was one who did not use a birch stick very much. And a bad teacher was one who used it a lot!

Narcissa quickly learned her ABC's. In school, she practiced writing them on a flat, smooth piece of slate stone. But she did not have chalk, as children do today. Back then, pupils wrote on their slates with a pencil that was also made of slate. After the teacher checked their work, they would erase the writing with a rag.

Narcissa also learned to do simple arithmetic. While the little children in the front row practiced writing letters and numbers, Narcissa's group did arithmetic problems. Narcissa almost always had the right answers. That made her happy. A pupil who wrote wrong answers had to stand in a corner of the room and wear a tall pointed hat. This was called the "dunce cap." All the children made fun of anybody who was sent to the dunce's corner.

The Prattsburg school did not have many books. But it did have a reading book called a primer. The primer had poems, stories, spelling lists, drawings, and sentences to read aloud.

The stories in the primer were used to teach reading *and* a lesson on how to behave.

Every minute of school time was spent learning something. However, the teacher did not give any homework. That is because she knew every child had many chores to do at home.

By the time Narcissa was ten, she could do just about all the jobs her mother did. And she was expected to do them well. Now Mrs. Prentiss could go off to visit a sick friend or do community work. She knew that Narcissa would take care of the house.

One of the jobs Narcissa enjoyed most was apple-drying. All through the autumn months, Mr. Prentiss and the children gathered apples from their orchard. Some of the fruit was put in the food cellar. This was a room built under the ground near the house. It was like a small underground cave, and it stayed cool all the time. There were no refrigerators in those days, but food stored in the cellar stayed in good condition for months.

Some of the apples were eaten right away. Some were pressed for their juice. The rest were dried. Every autumn afternoon, when Narcissa came home from school, she would prepare apples for drying. To do this, she cut out the cores and sliced the apples into thin rings. Then she took down the drying tray. The large, flat drying tray hung high on hooks near the fireplace.

34

The apple slices were set on the tray, and the tray was put back up on the hooks. The heat from the fire soon dried the apple slices. Once they were dried, the apple slices would not spoil, even if they weren't eaten for several months.

As soon as the slices were dry, Narcissa took them off the tray. Then she strung the apple rings on a long cord. When there was no room left on the cord for any more apple rings, she tied the ends of the cord. Then she hung the cord of slices in the shed behind the house. Any time the Prentisses wanted dried apples, there they were.

One of the jobs Narcissa liked least was making soap. Still, it had to be done. If it wasn't, the Prentiss family and their clothing would never be clean. What Narcissa hated about soap-making was the awful smell.

When Mr. Prentiss shot a bear, the fat was used to make soap. First, Narcissa started a fire outside the house. She set a huge iron pot on the burning wood. Then she threw a few chunks of the smelly, slippery fat into the pot. As the fat melted, she added more chunks to the pot. She kept doing this until the pot was full.

Soap-making took hours and hours. After all the fat was melted, Narcissa poured in firewood ashes. Then she stirred and stirred the greasy mixture with a long, wooden pole. It was hot and tiring work. But when Mrs. Prentiss praised Narcissa's soap, the young girl felt rewarded for every minute of her hard work.

By the time Narcissa was twelve, she was able to run a household. She cooked and baked, sewed and spun, made soap and candles and dyes, cleaned, fed the chickens, milked the cows, and took care of her little brothers and sisters.

In school, too, she had been a very good pupil. And on graduation day her teacher had many words of praise for Narcissa.

For most boys and girls of that time, schooling ended at about the age of twelve. But Narcissa was very smart, and her parents felt she should have more education. That same year, Mrs. Emma Willard opened a school for girls in Troy, New York. It was called the Female Seminary, and it was the first high school of its kind for girls in the United States.

Narcissa spent three joyful years at Mrs. Willard's school. She had great fun living there with other girls her age. And she enjoyed studying mathematics, science, poetry, and religion.

Sometimes Narcissa talked about her dreams of going west. But each time she did, she was told that such work was not for women. Instead of that, her friends said, she should become a teacher, as she so much wanted to.

"And who knows what may happen in the future?" her best friend said. "Perhaps one day there will be a need for an experienced teacher at a mission out West. Should that day come, Narcissa, you will be ready."

In 1824, when Narcissa was sixteen, she graduated from the Female Seminary. She spent the next eleven years teaching school in several towns near the Prentiss home. She was a good teacher, and she loved working with young people. Even so, she could not forget her dream.

Year after year, Narcissa wrote letters to the Missionary Board, asking to be sent out West. And year after year, the answer was the same: No.

Then she met Marcus Whitman. He was a doctor who had the same dream as Narcissa. Soon their friendship turned to love. Now both of them began writing to the Board, asking to be sent out West together. This time, in the winter of 1836, the answer was: "Yes. We would be pleased to have you join us, as husband and

wife. Indeed, the Oregon territory has need of doctors and teachers."

Narcissa and Marcus decided to get married right away. They hoped to reach Oregon before the next winter, so they had to leave almost immediately. That's because it took several months to travel across the country.

On February 18, 1836, right after their wedding, Narcissa and Marcus Whitman said good-by to their families and friends. And, that same day, they began their journey west.

The Whitmans joined another couple, Eliza and Henry Spalding, when they reached Cincinnati. Together they loaded supplies aboard the wagon that would take them across the desert plains and mountains of this rugged territory. A wagon such as this had never succeeded in crossing North America, but the Whitmans hoped to prove it could be done. They believed that if others knew of their success, they would be encouraged to join the Whitmans at their frontier settlement.

Indeed, the Spaldings and the Whitmans traveled a good part of the way by wagon. But, at last, the many dangerous river crossings and the blistering desert heat took their toll on the small wagon, and it was left behind. The rest of the trip was made on horseback and on foot.

The Whitmans were making history. Except for mountain men and fur trappers, only Indians lived in the northwest. In fact, Narcissa Whitman and Eliza Spalding were the first pioneer women to cross the Rocky Mountains. On July 4, 1836, the weary travelers reached the high ground of the Rockies, called the Continental Divide, in Wyoming. There is a monument at South Pass, Wyoming, to mark the spot where Narcissa passed that day.

In November 1836, the Whitmans finally reached the place where they would build their mission. It was a beautiful clearing on the Walla Walla River.

For the next eleven years, Narcissa's life was busy and happy. She taught reading and writing to Indian children, and she helped her husband care for the sick.

Narcissa also helped to make new settlers comfortable in this rough, but beautiful wilderness. For just as Marcus and Narcissa had hoped, when word of their successful journey reached home, other families decided to move west. Many pioneers followed the Whitmans' trail. And the Whitman settlement became a welcome stopping-off point for tired travelers. This stream of visitors kept Narcissa very busy. She put to use every skill she had learned as a young girl in Prattsburg.

Narcissa continued to do good works for both Indians and settlers. Then, on November 29, 1847, she and Marcus were killed by hostile Indians.

Narcissa Whitman was only thirty-nine years old when she died. But she did more for others in her lifetime than most people do in twice that time. A brave and good woman, she became a model for the thousands of pioneer women who followed her westward path.

Laura Gets Married

When Laura was only fifteen, she began teaching school. At first, the students made her nervous. But soon she was in charge. The job was not close to her home, so she lived away. Each weekend Almanzo gave her a ride home.

Laura married Almanzo Wilder when she was eighteen. In 1886, they had a daughter named Rose. She was named after the prairie flowers her mother loved. Almanzo wanted to be a farmer, but these were hard years for them. Their crops failed. Then Almanzo became very sick and almost died.

Laura was a teacher in a one-room school.

After a few years, the Wilder family moved to Missouri. Winters were mild there. They bought a farm with a little log house. Laura loved the apple trees on the farm. At last, she was settled in one place.

The Wilders worked hard on their farm. The land was rocky and hilly. Still, Laura loved it there. It was during these years that Laura told Rose stories of her early life on the prairie. She told what it was like to travel in a covered wagon. She told what it was like to live in a dugout house. She told what it was like when a blizzard hit.

Children from all over the United States wrote to Laura and asked about her life. She got so many letters that she decided to keep writing books to answer all the questions. Laura wrote eleven books about life on the prairie.

In 1957, Laura Ingalls Wilder died at the age of ninety. But her stories about the life she lived on the prairie are still alive. Today her books are still read by children all over the world.

Rose Wilder asked her mother to write about life on the prairie.

Rose grew up and became an author. She always remembered her mother's stories. Rose asked Laura to write these stories down. At the age of sixty-five, Laura Ingalls Wilder became an author.

She wrote her first children's book in between doing farm chores. It took her over a year to do this. But the time and work were worth it. Her first book, named *Little House in the Big Woods,* became a big hit.

The Wilders built this house next to the log house.

Laura signed many copies of her books for her readers.

Glossary

author   person who writes a book

blizzard   a winter storm with heavy snow and strong winds

crops   plants grown to be used as food

dugout   a house made by digging a hole in the side of a hill

fiddle   a violin; a musical instrument

prairie   flat land covered with tall grass but few trees

settle   to make a home in a place

sod   soil that has grass growing on it

starved   died of hunger